RUSSIA

By Donna Reynolds
and Kaitlyn Duling

EXPLORING WORLD CULTURES

Cavendish Square

Published in 2025 by Cavendish Square Publishing, LLC
2544 Clinton Street, Buffalo, NY 14224

Second Edition

Website: cavendishsq.com

Library of Congress Cataloging-in-Publication Data

Names: Duling, Kaitlyn, author. | Reynolds, Donna, 1976- author.
Title: Russia / Donna Reynolds and Kaitlyn Duling.
Description: Second edition. | Buffalo, NY : Cavendish Square Publishing, [2025] | Series: Exploring world cultures | Includes bibliographical references and index.
Identifiers: LCCN 2024027420 | ISBN 9781502672940 (library binding) | ISBN 9781502672933 (paperback) | ISBN 9781502672957 (ebook)
Subjects: LCSH: Russia (Federation)--Juvenile literature.
Classification: LCC DK510.23 .D58 2025 | DDC 947--dc23/eng/20240802
LC record available at https://lccn.loc.gov/2024027420

Writers: Kaitlyn Duling; Donna Reynolds (second edition)
Editor: Jennifer Lombardo
Copyeditors: Jill Keppeler and Danielle Haynes
Designer: Deanna Lepovich

The photographs in this book are used by permission and through the courtesy of: Cover AdaCo/Shutterstock.com; p. 4 Volodymyr Burdiak/Shutterstock.com; p. 5 Baturina Yuliya/Shutterstock.com; p. 6 Olga Gavrilova/Shutterstock.com; p. 7 DrAndY/Shutterstock.com; p. 8 Everett Collection/Shutterstock.com; p. 9 FedotovAnatoly/Shutterstock.com; p. 10 Konstantin Lenkov/Shutterstock.com; p. 11 Free Wind 2014/Shutterstock.com; p. 12 Seneline/Shutterstock.com; p. 13 FOTOGRIN/Shutterstock.com; p. 15 (top) ANDREI RASPUTIN/Shutterstock.com; p. 15 (bottom) Golden_Images/Shutterstock.com; p. 17 (top) FotograFFF/Shutterstock.com; p. 17 (bottom) Vladimir_Dresvyannikov/Shutterstock.com; p. 18 Viacheslav Lopatin/Shutterstock.com; p. 19 longtaildog/Shutterstock.com; p. 20 (left) elenovsky/Shutterstock.com; p. 20 (right) Petr Kahanek/Shutterstock.com; p. 21 Alexander A.Trofimov/Shutterstock.com; p. 22 Artsiom P/Shutterstock.com; p. 23 Lisa-Lisa/Shutterstock.com; p. 24 Atlantist Studio/Shutterstock.com; p. 25 Evgeniy Kalinovskiy/Shutterstock.com; p. 26 Tom Godfrey/Shutterstock.com; p. 27 Tatiana Zinchenko/Shutterstock.com; p. 29 (top) Alena Matrosova/Shutterstock.com; p. 29 (bottom) Tatiana Yashina/Shutterstock.com.

CPSIA compliance information: Batch #CW25CSQ: For further information contact Cavendish Square Publishing LLC at 1-877-980-4450.

Printed in the United States of America

CONTENTS

INTRODUCTION

Russia is the largest country by area in the world. It is so big that it stretches across two continents: Europe and Asia. However, most of it is **uninhabited**. The majority of Russians live in several cities in the western part of the country.

Many amazing animals live in Russia. Some are endangered, or at risk of dying out. Russia has laws that are meant to keep these animals safe. However, illegal hunting is a problem.

The endangered Siberian tiger is one of Russia's most famous animals.

Russia has a rich history and culture, or way of life. Russian authors have been popular around the world for a long time. Many Russians are proud of their country. However, a growing number of Russians are not happy with the way the government is doing things. These people are **protesting** in spite of the danger of being arrested. They want their country to be better to its own people and to people in other countries.

St. Basil's Cathedral is a famous church in Moscow, the capital of Russia.

GEOGRAPHY

Russia covers more than 6.6 million square miles (17.1 million square kilometers). It borders 14 countries and several bodies of water. Because it's so big, it has many different **climates**. To the far north is the tundra, which is very cold and dry, with few plants. Below that is the taiga, or northern forest. Farther south, the climate gets warmer. Near the Black Sea, it is almost tropical.

FACT!

One-eighth of all the land on Earth is in Russia.

One of the largest parts of Russia is the steppe, or grassland. Here, winters are cold and summers are warm.

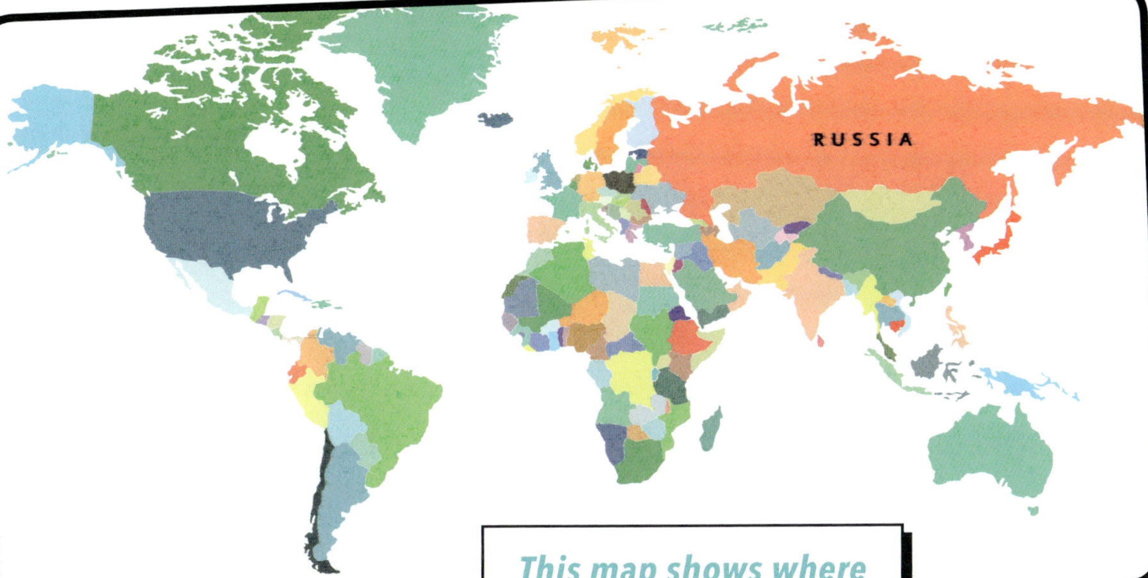

This map shows where Russia is in the world.

Within Russia, there are many geographical features. This includes Europe's two largest lakes: Ladoga and Onega. The country also has many rivers and mountains. The Ural Mountains divide Europe and Asia.

ALL AROUND RUSSIA

Russia's bordering countries are Poland, Lithuania, Norway, Finland, Estonia, Latvia, Belarus, Ukraine, Georgia, Azerbaijan, Kazakhstan, China, Mongolia, and North Korea. The country also touches the Arctic Ocean, Baltic Sea, Pacific Ocean, and Black Sea.

HISTORY

For much of its history, Russia was ruled by a leader called the czar (also spelled "tsar"). In 1917, a group called the Bolsheviks, led by Vladimir Lenin, took power. Lenin became a **dictator** and created the Union of Soviet Socialist Republics (USSR). It included Russia and 14 other countries.

Catherine the Great took power in 1762. Under her rule, education and art thrived.

FACT!

From 1947 to 1991, the USSR was in a "Cold War" with the United States. Neither country trusted the other, but no battles were fought between them.

After World War II (1939–1945), the USSR focused on space exploration. In 1961, Yuri Gagarin, shown here, became the first person in the world to go to space.

The USSR lasted until 1991. After that, Russia was a single country again. Vladimir Putin was elected president in 2000 and again in 2012. In 2022, Putin started a war with Ukraine. Many people believe his goal is to make Russia bigger, the way Lenin did.

BEFORE THE CZARS

Ivan the Terrible became Russia's first czar in 1547. He took control of the land that is now included in Russia. Before this time, many different groups fought for control of parts of Russia. These included the Greeks, the Huns, and the Khazars.

GOVERNMENT

In name, Russia is a **democracy**. There are different branches, or parts, of the government that are all supposed to have different powers. In reality, Russia is a dictatorship. Vladimir Putin controls everything. People who say no to him or speak out against him are often killed or put in prison. Putin claims he has nothing to do with this.

Most Russians disagree with Putin's decisions, especially his war with Ukraine. However, many are scared to speak out because of the danger of being killed or arrested.

In Russia, **LGTBQ+** people and many others are not safe. Protesting Putin's decisions can get people arrested. The news has to say that Putin is doing a good job. This means many Russians don't know exactly what their government is doing.

FACT!

Russians are allowed to vote, but many people believe Putin rigs the elections, or illegally changes the results.

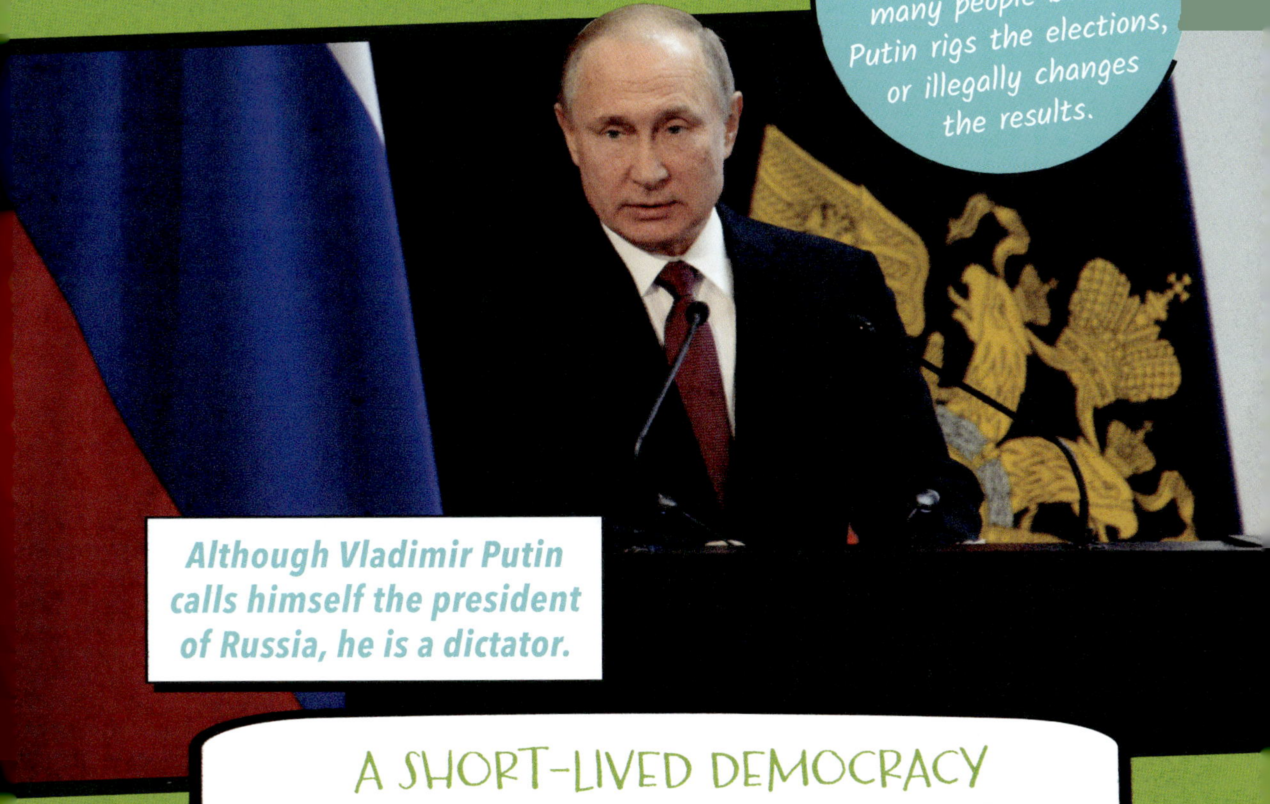

Although Vladimir Putin calls himself the president of Russia, he is a dictator.

A SHORT-LIVED DEMOCRACY

In 1991, Russia became a democracy. Presidents could serve for only two four-year terms consecutively, or in a row. At the end of Putin's second consecutive term in 2020, Russia passed a law that would let him stay in power until at least 2036.

THE ECONOMY

The Russian **economy** suffered in late 2022 and early 2023. Many countries have put **sanctions** on Russia because of the war in Ukraine. As the war has gone on, the economy has gotten a little better. There are now a lot of jobs for Russians in factories that make weapons.

FACT!
Russian money is called "rubles."

Many Russians are either fighting in the war or making items for it, such as these tanks.

COMMUNIST RUSSIA

When the Bolsheviks took over, they made Russia a Communist country. Under Communism, the government controls all the businesses.

The country is full of things people can use. It is especially rich in oil and gas. Other countries use these for energy, or power. It also has gold and aluminum. However, the sanctions mean Russia is not exporting, or selling, as much as it did before the war. Within the country, **inflation** is high. Many people have trouble affording the things they used to be able to buy.

Many Russian cities, such as St. Petersburg, look clean and beautiful. This makes it easier for people to believe the country has no problems.

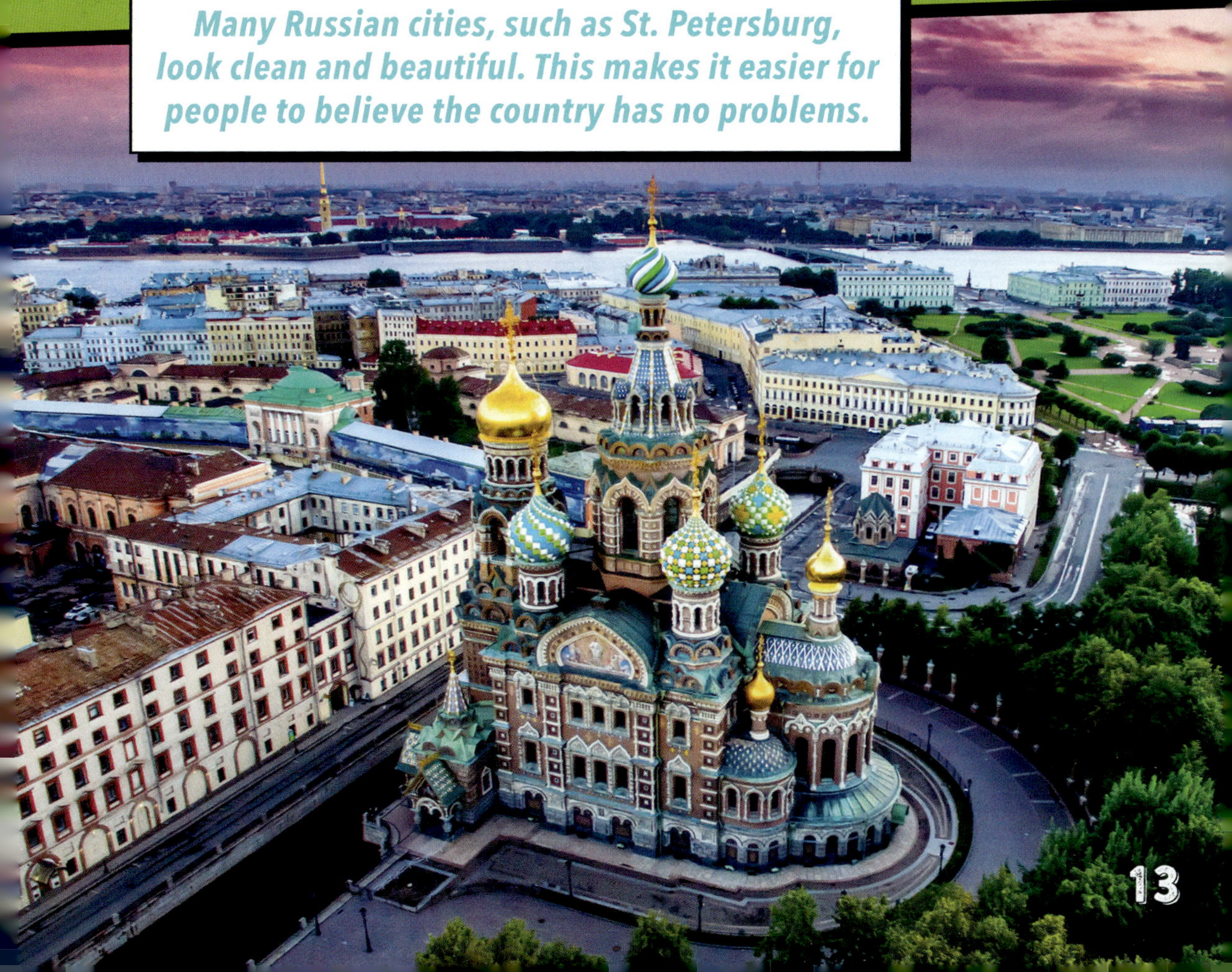

THE ENVIRONMENT

Russia has many environmental problems, or problems in its natural world. Loggers have cut down many trees, and forests are not kept safe.

Climate change is a problem all over the world, including Russia. For example, melting ice caused by climate change in Siberia, far in the north of Russia, has caused floods that wipe out people's homes.

Many countries are working on cutting back their use of fossil fuels. Russia, however, is focused on its war. It is using more fossil fuels to power its weapons factories. This is polluting, or dirtying, the air.

FACT!

Aside from making climate change worse, air pollution can make it hard for animals and people to breathe.

A HUMAN PROBLEM

Climate change is driven largely by human activities. Pollution from burning fossil fuels—such as oil, gas, and coal—is making the planet warmer. This is causing the climate to change in many different ways.

A type of weasel called a sable is very common in Russia, especially in the Ural Mountains and in the taiga.

There are only about 100 Amur leopards left in the world. Nearly all of them live in a protected area on the border between Russia and China.

THE PEOPLE TODAY

Russia has a population of more than 140 million people. About 75 percent of people live in cities in the European part of the country. There are nearly 200 **ethnic** groups in the country. The largest ethnic group, making up about 80 percent of the population, is Russian. Other groups include Tatars, Ukrainians, and Armenians. Tatars are the second-largest group. They make up about 4 percent of the population. Tatars come from early nomadic, or traveling, groups. Many are native to Crimea and the Volga area.

Russians are generally known for being kind to guests. They take their time making friends, but once they do, they treat their friends as if they are family.

MOVIES VS. REAL LIFE

In movies, Russians are often shown as very serious—sometimes even mean. In reality, many Russians enjoy joking and laughing with their friends and family.

These girls are wearing **traditional** Tatar clothing.

FACT!

The Russian ethnic group is similar to other ethnic groups that are native to Eastern Europe.

Traditional Russian clothing is still sometimes worn on special days. Most days, Russians wear the same kind of clothes Americans do.

LIFESTYLE

Life is very different for a Russian in the city than one in the country. In cities, most people live in apartment buildings. They get around using public transportation, such as the bus or subway. For fun, many enjoy reading and going to see plays. Many have jobs in weapons factories as well as stores, hospitals, or schools.

FACT!

In Siberia, many people make a living by herding reindeer.

This picture shows a subway station in Moscow.

In the countryside, people are much more spread out. They tend to live in wooden houses and spend a lot of time taking care of their land. Many make a living by trapping animals for their fur, fishing, and raising horses or cattle.

STRONG CONNECTIONS

Russians care a lot about keeping their friendships and family relationships strong. They believe it is better to work together than to try to do everything on their own.

In the far north, some people still live a nomadic lifestyle.

RELIGION

Most Russians follow the Russian Orthodox religion, or faith. This religion has played a huge part in Russian culture, history, and even government for hundreds of years. Even today, Vladimir Putin has made it clear that some of his choices as president have been in line with his religious beliefs.

FACT!

The word "orthodox" means "correct in teaching." Orthodox Christians consider their teachings to be the most true to the Christian religion.

Most Christians around the world use the Latin cross (right) as a sign of their faith. The Russian Orthodox church uses the Eastern cross (left), which has two extra bars on it.

There are also a few Roman Catholic and other Christian churches in Russia. Islam is the second-most popular religion in Russia. Some smaller ethnic groups such as Tatars and Chechens are mainly Muslim.

In Siberia, some people practice a type of religion called shamanism. This religion has been around since about 3300 BCE.

The iconic domes on Russian Orthodox churches are called "onion domes."

AN OLD RELIGION

Russian Orthodox Christianity is part of the Eastern Orthodox Church. This is a very old form of Christianity. Its members still generally follow the rules and beliefs put in place by Emperor Constantine in 325 CE.

LANGUAGE

Russia's official language is Russian. An official language is the one the government, schools, and businesses use. However, today there are more than 100 different languages spoken across the country!

FACT!
Astronauts are required to learn Russian before they can go to space.

The computer on the International Space Station (ISS) uses both English and Russian.

The Russian system of writing is called Cyrillic. Some of the letters look similar to Latin letters–the ones the English alphabet uses.

When Russia was brought together as one country years ago, many people continued to speak their native language. For example, Tatars have their own language, but they also speak Russian. Russian is also an official language in the former USSR countries of Belarus, Kyrgyzstan, and Kazakhstan.

English, German, and French are taught in Russian schools. Students are required to pick at least two. Older adults may know only one or two languages.

A GLOBAL LANGUAGE

Russian is the eighth-most spoken language in the world. There are about 254 million native speakers. Not all of them live in Russia.

ARTS AND FESTIVALS

Russia is well known for its arts, especially its books. Some of the most famous books in history are Russian, including *Crime and Punishment* by Fyodor Dostoevsky and *Anna Karenina* by Leo Tolstoy. Religious paintings are also an important part of the Russian art culture.

FACT!
Orthodox Christmas falls on January 7 rather than December 25.

One of the most ***unique*** *Russian crafts is the matryoshka, or nesting doll.*

The balalaika is a traditional Russian stringed instrument.

Russians also enjoy many different festivals. Some are religious, such as Orthodox Christmas. Others focus on art and food. Russian winters are famously long and gloomy, so the mid-winter festival gives Russians something to look forward to. They can go to markets selling handmade crafts, eat warm foods, and watch balalaika concerts.

THE NEW YEAR

New Year's Eve and New Year's Day are, combined, the biggest holiday in Russia. Families get together to exchange gifts. Cities put on large fireworks displays. Many people go out dancing on New Year's Eve.

FUN AND PLAY

Sports, especially soccer and hockey, are very popular in Russia. In Russia, there is a game called “bandy” that combines these two sports. Volleyball and skiing are also popular. In addition to sports, Russians like to play games. The video game *Tetris* was invented in Russia. More modern video games are also very popular, especially among kids and teens.

MIRACLE ON ICE

During the 1980 Winter Olympics, the U.S. hockey team beat the USSR team. The Americans called this the "Miracle on Ice" because the USSR team was known as the best in the world.

Chess is a popular game in Russia among people of all ages.

When they have free time, many Russians enjoy relaxing with a book, watching TV, or doing a craft, such as knitting. They may meet up with friends to go shopping or eat at a restaurant. Often, Russians will spend an entire day with their friends.

FACT!
When the weather is nice, many Russians enjoy camping.

Many city-dwelling Russians have country houses called dachas. Families spend a lot of time at their dacha in summer, working in the garden and enjoying the peace and quiet.

FOOD

There are many different kinds of Russian foods. Some, such as borscht, are popular all over the country. This is a beet soup that originally came from Ukraine. Others are found mainly in certain parts. For example, *shashlik* is the word for a meal that was first made by tribes living in the Caucasus Mountains. Shashlik is made by putting meat and vegetables on a wooden skewer, or stick, and cooking them over a fire.

Cabbage and pickled vegetables are common ingredients in many Russian dishes. These foods last a long time. Before grocery stores became common, such foods would have to keep Russians fed throughout the long winter.

FACT!

Borscht can be served hot, but it is more often served cold.

PELMENI

The national dish of Russia is called *pelmeni*. These are meat dumplings that are generally served with sour cream and butter. Sometimes they are eaten alone; other times, they are used as a soup ingredient.

A blini is a kind of pancake. It can be eaten with sweet or ***savory*** *toppings. These blinis are topped with caviar, or fish eggs. Caviar has been a favorite food among wealthy Russians for many years.*

Kvass is made from fermented bread. Honey, berries, or herbs are sometimes added to give it extra flavor. It is an especially popular summer drink.

GLOSSARY

climate: The weather over a long period of time.

democracy: A system of government in which people vote for their leaders.

dictator: A person who rules with total authority and often in a cruel or brutal manner.

economy: The way goods and services are made and sold.

ethnic: Of or relating to large groups of people who have the same cultural background and ways of life.

inflation: A continual rise in the price of goods and services.

LGBTQ+: Relating to a group made up of people who see themselves as a gender different from the sex they were assigned at birth or who want to be in romantic relationships that aren't only male-female. LGBTQ stands for lesbian, gay, bisexual, transgender, and queer or questioning.

protest: To speak out strongly against something. Also, an event in which people gather to show they do not like something.

sanction: A measure, often economic, used to punish or prevent action.

savory: Having a spicy or salty quality without sweetness.

traditional: Following what's been done for a long time.

uninhabited: Not lived in by people.

unique: Special or one of a kind.

FIND OUT MORE

Books

Edwards, Sue Bradford. *Russia*. Minneapolis, MN: Essential Library, 2023.

Marshall, Deb. *Russia*. New York, NY: Lightbox Learning Inc., 2023.

Van, R.L. *Russia*. Minneapolis, MN: Big Buddy Books, 2023.

Websites

BrainPOP: Cold War
www.brainpop.com/socialstudies/ushistory/coldwar
Learn more about what the Cold War was and what happened during those years.

Kiddle: Russia Facts for Kids
kids.kiddle.co/Russia
Learn more interesting facts about Russia.

Video

YouTube: My Nesting Doll Collection #0038
www.youtube.com/watch?v=HnDij14xXBA
Take an up-close look at a set of Russian nesting dolls.

Publisher's note to educators and parents: Our editors have carefully reviewed these websites to ensure that they are suitable for students. Many websites change frequently, however, and we cannot guarantee that a site's future contents will continue to meet our high standards of quality and educational value. Be advised that students should be closely supervised whenever they access the internet.

INDEX